Old John Brown, The Man Whose Soul Is Marching On

by

Walter Hawkins

Double 9 BOOKS

Old John Brown, The Man Whose Soul Is Marching On

by Walter Hawkins

ISBN: 978-93-64289-88-7

Published by

DOUBLE 9 BOOKS

2/13-B, Ansari Road
Daryaganj, New Delhi – 110002
info@double9books.com
www.double9books.com
Tel. 011-40042856

ABOUT THE AUTHOR

Walter Hawkins, the author of "Old John Brown: The Whole Man Whose Soul Is Marching On," was a historian and scholar focused on American history, particularly the abolitionist movement and figures central to that era. Unlike the well-known gospel singer of the same name, this Walter Hawkins dedicated his career to researching and writing about historical topics, offering in-depth analyses and biographies that shed light on significant individuals and events in American history. Hawkins' biography of John Brown examines the life, motivations, and impact of the controversial abolitionist who played a crucial role in the events leading up to the Civil War. The book aims to provide a comprehensive and nuanced portrayal of John Brown, exploring his personal convictions, actions, and the broader context of his times.

CONTENTS

PREFACE

This book is for busy people who have not the time to read at large upon the subject. Those who would adequately master all the bearings of the story here briefly told must read American history, for which facilities are rapidly increasing. As to John Brown himself, his friend F. B. Sanborn's LIFE AND LETTERS is a mine of wealth. To its pages the present writer is greatly indebted, and he commends them to others.

W. H.
Kilburn, May 1913.

CHAPTER I
WHY WE WRITE OUR STORY

There are few who have not a dim notion of John Brown as a name bound up with the stirring events of the United States in the period which preceded the Civil War and the emancipation of the slave. Many English readers, however, do not get beyond the limits of the famous couplet,

> John Brown's body lies mouldering in the grave,
> But his soul is marching on.

That statement is authentic in both its clauses, but it is interesting to learn what he did with the body before it commenced a dissolution which seems to have been regarded as worth recording. Carlyle says in his grimly humorous way of the gruesome elevation of the head of one of his patriotic heroes on Temple Bar, 'It didn't matter: he had quite done with it.' And we might say the same of the body which was hanged at Charlestown in 1859. In his devoutly fatalistic way John Brown had presented his body a living sacrifice to the cause of human freedom, and had at last slowly reached the settled opinion that it was worth more to the cause dead than alive. Such a soul, so masterful in its treatment of the body, was likely to march on without it. And it did in the years that followed, This Abolitionist raider, with a rashness often sublime in its devotion, precipitated the national crisis which issued in the Civil War and Emancipation.

There are lives of brave men which set us thinking for the most part of human power and skill: we watch bold initiators of some wise policy carrying their enterprise through with indomitable courage and inexhaustible patience, and we are lost in admiration of the hero. But there are other brave lives which leave us thinking more of unseen forces which impelled them than of their own splendid qualities. They never seem masters of destiny, but its intrepid servants. They shape events while they hardly know how or why; they seem to be rather driven by fate than to be seeking fame or power. They go out like Abraham, 'not knowing whither they go,' only that, like him, they have heard a call. Sometimes they sorely tax the loyalty of their admirers with their eccentricities and their defiance of the conventions of their age. Wisdom is only justified of these, her strange children, in the next generation. Prominent among such lives is that of John

Brown. The conscience of the Northern States on the question of slavery needed but some strong irritant to arouse it to vigorous action, and, the hanging of John Brown sufficed.

The institution of slavery became both ridiculous and hateful to multitudes because so good a man must be done to death to preserve it. The verdict of Victor Hugo, 'What the South slew last December was not John Brown, but slavery,' found an echo in many minds. And when the long, fierce conflict, through which Emancipation came, was begun, the quaint lines,

> John Brown's body lies mouldering in the grave,
> But his soul is marching on,

became one of the mightiest of the battle-songs which urged the Federal hosts to victory. His name kindled the flame of that passion for freedom which made the cause of the North triumphant, and there was awe mingled with the love they bore his memory. Perhaps no man had been oftener called with plausible reason a fool; but those who knew the single-hearted devotion to a great cause of this ready victim of the gallows came reverently to think of him as 'God's fool.' When they sang 'John Brown died that the slave might be free' they were singing more than a record of John Brown's generous motive; it was a record of one of God's strange counsels. 'For God chose the foolish things of the world that He might put to shame the things that are strong, and the base things of the world, and the things that are despised, did God choose, yea, and the things that are not, that He might bring to nought the things that are, that no flesh should glory before God.' Verily, then, it might seem worth while to set the story of John Brown in such a plain, brief form as to make it available for busy folk who have no time to read longer accounts of him. If it sets some thinking of the ways of God rather than admiring John Brown, that will be just what he would have ardently wished who desired always that God should be magnified in his body, whether in the fighting which he never loved and never shirked, or the hanging which he often foresaw and never feared.

CHAPTER II
CHILDHOOD AND THE VOW

The birth of John Brown is recorded in the following laconic style by his father in a little autobiography he wrote for his children in the closing days of his life. 'In 1800, May 8, John was born one hundred years after his great-grandfather; nothing else very uncommon.' In the year mentioned the family were living at Torrington, Connecticut, whence they shortly removed to Ohio, then the haunt of the Red Indian. They were of the pioneer farming class, which has supplied so many of the shapers of American history. The one great honour in their pedigree was that they descended from a man of the MAYFLOWER—Peter Brown, a working carpenter who belonged to that famous ship's company. We might say, indeed, that the story of John Brown flows from the events of 1620, the year of the MAYFLOWER. Two landings on the American coast that year were destined to be memorable. In August a Dutch vessel disembarked the first cargo of imported slaves—twenty of them; and that day Slavery struck deep root in the new land. And in November of that same year the MAYFLOWER, with her very different cargo of brave freemen, dropped anchor in Cape Cod Bay. The stream of ill results from that first landing and the stream of Puritan blood, generous in its passion for liberty, that flowed unimpoverished from Peter Brown through generations of sturdy ancestors—these are the streams destined to meet turbulently and to supply us with our story. Owen Brown, the father of John, thus testifies to his own fidelity to the tradition of liberty. 'I am an Abolitionist. I know we are not loved by many. I wish to tell how I became one. Our neighbour lent my mother a slave for a few days. I used to go out into the field with him, and he used to carry me on his back, and I fell in love with him.' There we have the clue to the history of the household of the Browns for the next two generations. They FELL IN LOVE With the despised negro, and this glorious trait passed like an heritage from generation to generation.

There is a letter extant which supplies us with the best information on John Brown's own boyhood. It was written for a lad in a wealthy home where he stayed in later days, who had asked him many questions about his experiences in early life. He humorously calls it a 'short story of a certain boy of my acquaintance I will call John.' A few extracts will reveal his character in the forming. Here, for instance, you may trace the conscientiousness (often morbid) which was so marked a feature in his later days. 'I cannot tell you of anything in the first four years of John's life worth mentioning save that at that early age he was tempted by three large brass pins belonging to a girl who lived in the family, and stole them. In this he was detected by his mother; and after having a full day to think of the wrong, received from her a thorough whipping.' He adds, 'I must not neglect to tell you of a very foolish and bad habit to which John was somewhat addicted. I mean, telling lies, generally to screen himself from blame or from punishment. He could not well endure to be reproached, and now I think had he been oftener encouraged to be entirely frank, by MAKING FRANKNESS A KIND OF ATONEMENT for some of his faults, he would not have had to struggle so long with this mean habit.'

A story is told of John's schooldays which is an amusing and quite characteristic instance of his ethical eccentricities. For a short time he and his younger brother Salmon were at a school together, and Salmon was guilty of some offence which was condoned by the master. John had serious concern for the effect this might have upon his brother's morals, and he sought the lenient teacher and informed him that the fault was much deprecated by their father at home, and he was sure castigation there would have been inevitable. He therefore desired it should be duly inflicted, as otherwise he should feel compelled to act as his father's proxy. Finding discipline was still lax, he proceeded with paternal solemnity to administer it himself. His brother acknowledged that this was done with reluctant fidelity! Truly the moral instincts of the family were worthy of their Puritan ancestry.

Although naturally self-conscious and shy, his precociousness in boyhood, bringing him into association, as it did, with much older folk, bred a somewhat arrogant manner. The rule he exercised over younger members of the family also made him somewhat domineering, a fault which he diligently sought to correct in later life. At fifteen he had become a miniature man of business and was driving cattle on long journeys with all the confidence of mid-age. The letter from which we have already quoted has one or two more passages which may enlighten us as to his rearing. Still writing in the third person, he says, 'John had been taught from earliest childhood to fear God and keep His commandments, and though quite sceptical he had always by turns felt much doubt as to his future well being. He became to some extent a convert to Christianity, and ever after a firm believer in the divine authenticity of the Bible. With this book he became very familiar, and possessed a most unusual memory of its entire contents.' Here are hints as to his early pursuits: 'After getting to Ohio in 1805, he was for some time rather afraid of the Indians and their rifles, but this soon wore off, and he used to hang about them quite as much as was consistent with good manners and learned a trifle of their talk. His father learned to dress deer-skins, and at six years old John was installed a young Buck-skin. He was, perhaps, rather observing, as he ever after remembered the entire process of deer-skin dressing, so that he could at any time dress his own leather, such as squirrel, racoon, cat, wolf, and dog skins, and also learned to make whiplashes, which brought him some change at times, and was of considerable service in many ways. He did not become much of a scholar. He would always choose to stay at home and work hard rather than be sent to school, and during the warm season might generally be seen barefooted and bareheaded, with buck-skin breeches suspended often with one leather strap over his shoulder, but sometimes with two. To be sent off through the wilderness alone to very considerable distances was particularly his delight; in this he was often indulged, so that by the time he was twelve years old he was sent off more than a hundred miles with companies of cattle. He followed up with tenacity whatever he set about so long as it answered his general purpose, and thence he rarely failed in some good degree to effect the things he undertook.'

'From fifteen years and upward he felt a good deal of anxiety to learn, but could only read and study a little, both for want of time and on account of inflammation of the eyes. He managed by the help of books, however, to make himself tolerably well acquainted with common arithmetic and surveying, which he practised more or less after he was twenty years old.' 'John began early in life to discover a great liking to fine cattle, horses, sheep, and swine; and as soon as circumstances would enable him, he began to be a practical shepherd—it being a calling for which, in early life, he had a kind of enthusiastic longing, together with the idea that as a business it bade fair to afford him the means of CARRYING OUT HIS GREATEST OR PRINCIPAL OBJECT.'

Here we touch the keynote of this life of manifold outward occupations, but of one consuming desire. That PRINCIPAL OBJECT filled his horizon even in childhood. He loved to tell how, like his father before him, he fell captive to the slave's dumb plea and pledged his whole strength to the chivalrous task of breaking his fetters. It happened on this wise. In those long journeys he was allowed to take, he was the 'business guest' of a slave-owner, who was pleased with his resourcefulness at such an age. He was the object of curious attention, and was treated as 'company' at table. On the estate was a young negro just his own age, and as intelligent as he. Young John struck up an acquaintance with him, and could not fail to contrast the fashion in which he himself was pampered with the way the young darkie was coarsely treated with scant fare and ill-housing. His frequent thrashings seemed to bruise young John's spirit as much as they did his flesh. They were not always administered with the orthodox whip, but with a shovel or anything else that came first to hand. Young John pondered long upon this contrast, and tells us how the iniquity of slavery was borne in upon his young heart, and he was drawn to this little coloured playmate, who had neither father nor mother known to him. The Bible was the final court of appeal in the Brown family, and the verdict of that court was that they two—the slave and the guest—were brothers, so henceforth the instinct of fraternal loyalty drew young John to 'swear eternal war with slavery.' That vow, never recanted or forgotten, became the text of his life. It interprets all his vagaries and reconciles what else were hopeless inconsistencies. It was a devout obsession which made him a wanderer all his days, and in the end carried him to prison and to death. To a child a great call had come, and a child's voice had replied, 'Speak, Lord, Thy servant heareth.' And ears and heart tingled at messages that seemed to come from the Unseen.

CHAPTER III
THE LONG WAITING-TIME

For over thirty years did this man both 'hope and quietly wait for the salvation of the Lord' to come for the slaves of his land. The interval is full of interest for those who care to watch the development of a life-purpose. Only for three, or four years was he destined to figure in the eyes of the world. Those years, as we shall hereafter see, were crowded with events; but for a generation he felt an abiding conviction of impending destiny.

There is something fateful about the constant indications of this spirit of readiness. His commercial pursuits were multifarious, but none of them was greatly successful. At Hudson, Ohio, till 1825, and afterwards at Richmond, Pennsylvania, he was tanner, land-surveyor, and part of the time postmaster. He became skilful at his father's business of tanning, but is a typical Yankee in the facility with which he turns his hand to anything.

From 1835 to 1839 he was at Franklin, Ohio, where we find him adding to his former occupations the breeding of horses, and also dabbling in land speculation, with the result that he became bankrupt. But when he failed in business he set to work to pay his debts in full. His death found him still striving to achieve that end. He was regarded as whimsical and stubborn, yet through years of struggle, endeavour, and even failure he was known as trusty and honourable.

From 1841 to 1846 he lived at Richfield, Ohio, where he took to shepherding and wool-dealing, which he continued in 1849 at Springfield, Massachusetts. He seems to have developed much capacity for wool-testing. When he came to England with a cargo of wool, some English dealers sought to practise a fraudulent joke upon his quick fingers. They stripped a poodle of the best of his fleece and handed it to the oracular Yankee with the inquiry, 'What would you do with that wool?' But there was wisdom in him down to the finger-ends, for he rolled it there, and in a moment handed it back with the confounding retort, 'Gentlemen, if you have any machinery in England for working up dog's hair I would advise you to put this into it.'

Had he known how to sell wool as well as he knew how to test it; had he known how to sell his sheep as well as he knew hundreds of sheep faces apart, and like a diviner could interpret their inarticulate language; had he been as apt upon the market as he was upon the farm, he might have made money. As it was, there was never more than enough for the wants of a severely plain household life.

But this business record was (and herefrom its frequent misfortune may have largely proceeded) in no wise the history of John Brown. We must catch, if we can, indications of the unfolding of his soul, and of the inward preparation for what he felt was his divine destiny; and these may best be gathered as we watch the simple home life of the family. At an early age, while residing at Hudson, Ohio, he married his first wife, Dianthe Lusk; and though he was but twenty years of age, his was no rash choice. A description by one who had been brought up with her may be fitly quoted: 'Plain but attractive, because of a quiet amiable disposition, sang beautifully, almost always sacred music; she had a place in the wood not far from the house where she used to go alone to pray.' John Brown, servant as he already accounted himself of the Invisible Powers, is drawn to one who thus communes with the Unseen. She will have sympathy with his moral aims and a source of strength when he may be absent from her in pursuit of them. The sketch proceeds, 'She was pleasant but not funny; she never said what she did not mean.' Here, truly, was the wife for a man in dead earnest and who could keep a boyish oath even unto death. For twelve years she proved a good comrade, and of the seven children of this marriage five survived, from whom testimonies concerning the domestic life are forthcoming.

The wife who succeeded her (Mary Ann Day) seems to have been no less a help-meet in his enterprises. Thirteen children, many of whom died young, were the off-spring of this second marriage, so that in a hereditary sense the soul of John Brown may be said to have marched on.

He infected all his children with his passionate love of liberty. Many are his cares for their spiritual welfare. Some of them sorely tried his patience by their aloofness from the Christian conventions that were dear to him; he yearns over their souls as he fears their experience of the inner working of grace is not as his own, but they swerved not in their allegiance to the cause of the slave. Let us avail ourselves of some of their memories of their remarkable father. How early the house became a city of refuge for the runaway negro we learn from the eldest son, who tells us he can just recollect a timid knock at the door of the log cabin where they lived. A fugitive slave and his wife were there, for they had heard that there were a couple residing in the house who loved the negro and would lend him a rescuing hand. They were speedily made to know they were welcome, and the negress, relieved of her last fear, takes young John in a motherly fashion upon her knee and kisses him. He almost instinctively scampers off to rub the black from his face. Returning, he watches his mother giving them supper. Presently father's extraordinarily quick ear detects the sound of horsehoofs half a mile away; weapons are thrust into the hands of the terrified pair, and they are taken out to the woody swamps behind the house to lie in hiding. Father then returns, only to discover that it is a false alarm, whereupon he sallies forth to bring them into shelter and warmth once more, and tells the assembled family on their arrival how he had difficulty in the dark in recognizing the hiding-place and really discovered them at length by hearing the beating of their frightened hearts. No wonder. Quick as any faculty he had was that of hearing a slave's heart beat. Had it not been for that keen instinct there would have been no tale to tell of John Brown.

The daughter says her earliest memory is of her father's great arms about her as he sang to her his favourite hymn:

> Blow ye the trumpet, blow
> The gladly solemn sound:
> Let all the nations know
> To earth's remotest bound.
> The year of Jubilee is come,
> Return, ye ransomed sinners, home.

Then, ceasing, he would tell her with heart brimming with tenderness of poor little black children who were slaves. What were slaves? she wanted to know. And he was ready enough to tell her of those who were riven from father and mother and sold for base coin, whom in some States it was illegal to teach their A B C, but quite lawful to flog; and then the daughter would be asked, by way of application to his moving discourse, if she would like some of them to come some time and share her home and food.

Thus continually to that rising family there was unfolded the horror of the slavery system. That horror had faded in the minds of many in the Northern States whose ancestry had held freedom dear; while in the Southern States, for the most part, the possession of your fellow creatures as if they were so much farm stock had become too familiar a feature of common life to evoke any conscientious misgiving, much less shame. The enormous additions to the cotton trade had made slave labour increasingly gainful, and the capital invested in this living property was immense. Careful rearing of slaves for the market as well as their purchase brought wealth to many, and fierce was the resentment when any one publicly criticized the institution. There was by no means an absence of humane regard far the wellbeing of the negroes; a kind of patriarchal tenderness towards them was distinctly 'good form.' But there was the deadly fact that they were human goods and chattels, with no civil rights worth mentioning—for laws in their defence were practically worthless, seeing they could not appear as witnesses in the court. Public whipping-houses were provided for the expeditious correction of the refractory, and a mere suspicion of intent to escape was legal justification for the use of the branding-irons upon their flesh. If they did contrive to escape there were dogs bred on purpose to hunt them down. If the slave resisted his master's will he might be slain, and the law would not graze the master's head. Domestic security he had none, for wife might be wrenched from husband or child from mother according to the state of the market. And, strangest of all to our ears, the pulpits of the South extolled slavery as appointed of Heaven, and solemnly quoting the prophecy that Ham should be the servant of his brethren, the pulpiteer would ask who would dare to resist the will of God Most High? Not content to hold their views tenaciously, the slave-holders and their followers dealt out threatenings and slaughter to all who by lip or pen opposed them. The household of Brown pondered all this invasion of the great natural right of freedom, and with one accord pined for the opportunity of checking, or, it might be, ending it.

It is on record how they were taught to repeat their father's vow. It was in 1839, when they were living at Franklin, Ohio, that he called them around him, and on bended knee declared the secret mission with which, he believed, High Heaven had charged him—to labour by word or sword, by any means opportunity might offer, for the overthrow of slavery, which he believed to be the very citadel of evil in America. 'Swear, children, swear,' said he; and from that little group in the log house there went up an appeal for a blessing upon their oath—an oath which they could truly protest was likely to bring nought to them but peril, disaster, and, perchance, death, but which they were well assured must bring glory to Eternal God. And so their oath was registered in heaven.

For many years it was only in indirect ways they could promote their end. Early they gave themselves to help the tentative endeavours that were often on foot to educate those slaves who did make good their escape, and especially to train them to independent agriculture, so that evidence might be afforded that they could use their liberty to good purpose, and become useful citizens. The Browns were always active in promoting such apprenticeship to freedom.

Two scenes reveal the temper of this united house. The first is at Franklin, where in the Congregational Church there are revival services being conducted, in which the Episcopalians and Methodists are uniting with their neighbours under the guidance of a fervent evangelist. The folk are greatly wrought upon, and are looking for an outpouring of divine grace. Among the large assemblies are many coloured folk, some free and some runaway slaves. The darkies are directed by judicious deacons to seats reserved for them near the door, where they will not vex the eyes of the worshipping whites. John Brown has swift argument within him as in his boyish days: 'Has God—their Father and ours—set any line betwixt His children? Is He a respecter of persons? And, if not, can we expect reasonably an outpouring of His grace while in this ungracious manner we are thwarting Him? We shall bar the blessing we seek.' Rising to his feet, he denounces the distinction in God's House, then, turning to his own family, who were accustomed to obey him, and whom he knew agreed with him, he bade them rise and take the seats near the door while the negroes came and took theirs near the front. Nothing loth, both parties did as they were told, to the confusion of the pious community. Next day pastor and deacons waited upon the refractory member—John Brown—to 'labour with him,' as the old church chronicle has it, upon his grave indecorum. But they found themselves belaboured with passages from Old Testament and New, and sundry stout doctrines of the Christian faith, till they retired discomfited, in their hearts delivering him to Satan that he might learn not to blaspheme. But Satan would have none of him, we are sure.

Another instance of the same devotion to the cause of freedom belongs to rather later days when they had removed to Springfield, Massachusetts. There they lived with their wonted simplicity, but it had been the fond design of mother and daughter to furnish the parlour in due course. The moment had arrived when the domestic finances seemed to allow of this modest luxury, but already John Brown had designs of another removal to North Elba, New York, where an estate was being occupied by escaped slaves under the patronage of Gerrit Smith, a wealthy Abolitionist. At this juncture he calls his family together and asks for their mind as to whether they should now furnish the parlour with their savings or retain them for the help of these black settlers who require clothes and other equipment as they start their new life of independence. The blood of the Browns flows as one stream, and the ready response of all is 'Save the money, father.'

His favourite books were well known by the children—JOSEPHUS, Plutarch's LIVES, NAPOLEON AND HIS MARSHALS, LIFE OF OLIVER CROMWELL, Baxter's SAINTS' REST, Bunyan's PILGRIM'S PROGRESS, and Henry ON MEEKNESS. What a significant medley of peace and war—the wolf and the lamb—Napoleon and Henry on Meekness side by side! But dearest ever was the Book which had been the oracle in his father's house—itself the Book of battles and yet the gospel of peace, the sacred charter of man's liberties and yet the holy statute book for man's government—the Bible. Swift paternal correction was there for any misquotation from that

Book; it was a Book not to be lightly paraphrased, but LEARNED AND OBEYED. In his own Bible there are pencillings that reveal at once the secret springs of his strange, and to outward seeming, erratic life. Thus these passages are marked: 'Remember them that are in bonds, as bound with them.' 'Whoso stoppeth his ear at the cry of the poor, he also shall cry and shall not be heard.' 'Whoso mocketh the poor reproacheth his Maker.' 'He that hath pity upon the poor lendeth unto the Lord.'

Above all passages, perhaps, was this quoted—Isa. lviii. 6: 'Is not this the fast that I have chosen, to loose the bands of wickedness, to undo the heavy burdens, and to let the oppressed go free, and that ye break every yoke? Is it not to deal thy bread to the hungry, and that thou bring the poor that are cast out to thy house?' If ever man kept that chivalrous fast before the Lord it was John Brown.

The last stage in what we may call the long preparation of John Brown for the prominent labours of his life reveals still further how the passionate love of the cause of liberty burned as a fire in the bones of this family. They were attracted by the proposal of Gerrit Smith, to celebrate the passing of West Indian Emancipation with the offer of 100,000 acres of his wild land in the north of New York State for coloured families to settle upon. Eager for the success of the experiment, Brown and his sons were prepared to start pioneering in the new region, so as to be near at hand to encourage and assist the new settlers. Prepared to choose their location as they deemed the exigencies of the great cause demanded, they settled at North Elba in what was then a wilderness in Essex county, and commenced to live a life of sterner simplicity than before, hewing in the forests, and clearing with axe and fire the land which they then proceeded to cultivate, obtaining food and clothes as those must who have neither store nor tailor near. There, with one room beneath that served by day, and two rooms overhead that served by night, they lived, and not discontentedly, for if there was little space or grandeur within there was plenty without; and John Brown, who was no mere conqueror of Nature, but a lover of her beauty, revelled in the glories of that untamed land, with its mountains wooded to their summits, with its frowning gorges and rushing torrents and its richly scented air. Best of all there were black settlers around whom they could help and thus forward their life-work, proving that the race they vowed should be free could appreciate and justify the boon.

CHAPTER IV
HOW THE CALL CAME

Thus, then, did this family live their life of preparation. But eventful days were at hand, and John Brown felt that his real life-work had yet to come. 'I have never,' he said, 'for twenty years made any business arrangement that would prevent me at any time from answering the call of the Lord. I have kept my affairs in such a condition that in two weeks I could wind them up and be ready to obey that call, permitting nothing to stand in the way of duty, neither wife, children, nor worldly goods; whenever the time should come, I was ready.' Now truly it seemed as if 'God's judgements' were to be abroad in the earth, as if He was 'travelling in the greatness of His strength, mighty to save' the oppressed; as if 'the Day of Vengeance' were in His heart, and the 'Year of His redeemed was come'; and, said John Brown's heart, 'He shall find one loyal henchman; I am ready.'

John Brown's call seemed to come after this wise. The enrolment of each New State in the Union was the occasion of fierce contention as to whether the territories should be free or whether slavery should be permitted. Each party had sought at such junctures to score an advantage, for the balance was often a very fine one between them.

The spirit of compromise had from the earliest days prevailed upon the thorny question. Washington was against slavery. Statesmen like Adams, Franklin, Madison, and Munroe had opposed it; but others had been willing to purchase the preservation of Union by concessions to the South, and toleration had been their consistent policy.

The Missouri compromise in 1820 had apparently settled the question as to the new State of Kansas, for all future States north of the latitude 36d 30m were to be free. But at the enrolment of Kansas the slave party circumvented this statute, and ensured local option for the State upon this matter. In 1854 the new State of Kansas proceeded to determine for itself once for all by popular election the grave question whether she was to be a Slave or a Free State. But in these young States, which were being almost daily reinforced by new residents, each at once entitled to vote, the slave party saw a rare opportunity for the manufacture of faggot votes. What was to hinder the inhabitants of Missouri, the neighbouring State—who were slavery men—from going over in a body and voting! Couldn't men migrate and change their minds? Scandalous, you say. It was. But the scandal was actually perpetrated. None other than the acting Vice-President of the United States advised this course, and he found many ready to improve upon his instructions. One official stated: 'To those who have qualms of conscience as to violating laws, State or National, I say the time has come when such impositions must be disregarded, since your rights and property are at stake. And I advise you one and all to enter every election district in Kansas and vote at the point of the bowie-knife and, the revolver.'

Thus, a thousand strong, with two cannon in their procession, the armed ruffians went to vote at an election out of their own State. If brave election judges protested—and some did, in spite of cocked pistols at their heads (like true lawyers ready to die for justice' sake)—and required the mob to establish their claims, they were overpowered; the ruffians seized the ballot-boxes, and in the end there were 4,908 votes cast, though there were only 1,410 genuine voters in the State. Such was the deliberate report of a committee years after. The Legislature thus elected met and were suffered to make a Statute Book for the young State. Penalties of imprisonment and death were liberally appointed for all who should dare to resist the institution of slavery.

With such legislation to shield their lawlessness, ruffians belonging to the class of 'mean whites' commenced a series of barbarous outrages in the interests of the slave-holders—a series sickening to contemplate. Two instances may be quoted which are typical:

A ruffian bets that he will scalp an Abolitionist in true Indian fashion, and rides out in search of his prey. A gentleman known to be opposed to slavery is met in a gig and shot; and, taking his scalp, the drunken fiend rides back, and producing the promised spoil, claims his due.

Another leader of the Free-State men is surrounded by these desperate ruffians, and his skull and brain are cloven with a hatchet. In fiendish glee they dance upon the almost breathless man, who vainly pleads, 'Do not abuse me, I am dying.' The only response is a shower of tobacco juice from their filthy lips into his pleading eyes. With his last breath he says, 'It is in a good cause,' and so dies—slaughtered because he dared to say others should share in his right of liberty. True, dying man, the cause is good and will triumph, though thou and many others die first!

Such scenes roused the ire of the long-suffering Free-State men of Kansas. Redress there was none, save in their own right arm, for, as Emerson says, 'A plundered man might take his case to the court and find the ring-leader who has robbed him dismounting from his own horse and unbuckling his knife to sit as judge.'

They were not without allies. There might be no government aid from Washington, but throughout the North were men who loved the cause of Abolition better than their own ease, and they came in ever-increasing numbers. Amongst them were several of Brown's upgrown sons, followed by their father, ready to settle in this new State, where they might turn the tide of public opinion in favour of Freedom.

Thus slowly the ranks of the righteous lovers of liberty were replenished, and they began to form into bands for mutual protection, farming and soldiering by turns as necessity dictated.

Some of John Brown's Northern friends, who knew the stuff of which he was made, and saw that if Freedom had no blow struck on her behalf she would be driven by outrage-mongers out of Kansas, equipped him with money and rifles, or, as they had come to be called, 'Beecher Bibles'—a tribute to Henry Ward Beecher's ardent championship of advanced views upon the slavery question.

On October 6, 1855, he arrived at Osawatomie, and we find him writing cheery words to his brave second wife and their family whom he had left, telling them to hope in God and comfort one another, humbly trusting they may meet again on God's earth, and if not—for his vow is 'to the death'—that they may meet in God's heaven. Of that second wife—heroine in obscurity, sharer of the oath which ever knit the household in one, mother of thirteen children—we might say much, but her spirit breathes in these words she speaks concerning her solitary days:

'That was the time in my life when all my religion, all my philosophy, and all my faith in God's goodness were put to the test. My husband was away from home, prostrated by sickness; I was helpless from illness; in one week three of my little ones died of dysentery—this but three months before the birth of another child. Three years after this sad time another little one, eighteen months old, was burned to death. Yet even in these trials God upheld me.'

Such was the wife who, while John Brown fought for liberty, grudged him not to such a cause, and patiently trained others who should bear his name worthily in days to come.

CHAPTER V
BIBLE AND SWORD

John Brown was now at his work; no longer the mere fingers, but the soul of him had found a task. He set before himself this object, to free Kansas from the slave-holders' grip.

The Free-State men had met and agreed to pay no taxes to a Legislature illegally elected. They organized a rival government, and brought themselves into violent antagonism to the Federal Authorities at Washington—for President Pierce and his Cabinet, which included the renowned Jefferson Davis, backed the pro-slavery Legislature and its following of ruffians. The town of Lawrence, which the Free Staters held, was taken and pillaged by a wild mob under the leadership of the United States Marshal, and we find the Browns in a company marching to its relief. There was much skirmishing, during which two of Brown's sons were taken prisoners. Only the constant vigilance and undaunted courage of a few desperately bold men kept heart in the lovers of liberty. But they (often led by John Brown) escaped the government officials who sought to arrest them and sped to the help of those who were marked as the victims of the marauders. So slowly did the Federal Authorities awake to the situation that for a time there seemed little protection to be expected for persecuted lovers of liberty.

We must now form some estimate of the two sides in this irregular warfare in which John Brown all through the summer of 1856 was so prominently engaged.

On the one hand were those whom the slave-holders relied upon for the most part to do their dirty work—ruffians, many of them from the neighbouring State; men who did not work, but who lived a wild life—not cultivating a tract of land around their rude dwelling-place like honest settlers, but fishing, shooting, and thieving for a living—preferring the atmosphere of a Slave State as more favourable to their life of lawlessness and plunder, and finding inspiration in the whisky-bottle for such deeds of devilry as have been described.

Upon the other side, waging a guerilla warfare—for little else was possible against enemies who preferred sneaking outrages to pitched battles—were little companies of some score or two. Captain John Brown's company was ever to the fore. He felt that outrage had gone far enough unchecked, and that it was time honest men took the aggressive and struck terror into cowards' hearts. They were not without fierceness, but it was the fruit of honest anger. Rifles in their judgement went not ill with Bible-reading and prayer—but we have heard of such before. Armed Roundheads and Scotch Covenanters combined prayer with sword exercise. In this camp, morning and evening prayers were an institution; uncivil treatment of prisoners was a gross offence; no intoxicating liquors were permitted. One by-law runs: 'All profane, vulgar, or ungentlemanly talk shall be discountenanced.' What! do these rough men set themselves up to be gentlemen! Yes, according to Emerson's own meaning when he says of Brown's supporters:

'All gentlemen, of course, are on his side. I do not mean by "gentlemen" people of scented hair and perfumed handkerchiefs, but men of gentle blood and generosity, "fulfilled with all nobleness," who, like the Cid, give the outcast leper a share of their bed; like the dying Sidney, pass the cup of cold water to the wounded soldier who needs it more. For what is the oath of gentle blood and knighthood! What but to protect the weak and lowly against the strong oppressor! Nothing is more absurd than to complain of this sympathy, or to complain of a party of men united in opposition to slavery. As well complain of gravity or the ebb of the tide. Who makes the Abolitionist! The slave-holder. The sentiment of mercy is the natural recoil which the laws of the universe provide to protect mankind from destruction by savage passions. And our blind statesmen go up and down, with committees of vigilance and safety, hunting for the origin of this new heresy. They will need a very vigilant committee, indeed, to find its birthplace, and a very strong force to root it up. For the arch-abolitionist, older than Brown, and older than the Shenanndoah Mountains, is Love, whose other name is Justice—which was before Alfred, before Lycurgus, before Slavery, and will be after it.'

John Brown and, at one time, six of his sons were in the company. Many were rejected who offered for service, not for lack of physical stature, but moral. 'I would rather,' said John Brown, 'have the smallpox, yellow fever, and cholera all together in my camp than a man without principles. It is a mistake to think that bullies are the best fighters. Give me God-fearing men—men who respect themselves; and with a dozen of them, I will oppose a hundred of these ruffians.' These are the men, then, who were found in Kansas woods, with bare heads and unkempt locks, in red-topped boots and blue shirts, taking their hasty meals or fitful sleep, their horses tied to the tree-trunks ready for swift mounting at the first signal of danger. No sounds of revelry betray their hiding-place; the spirit of the man in their midst, with Puritan nobility in his rugged face, and a strange, awe-inspiring unworldliness in his talk, has entered into them. No novice is he in the affairs of either world—this or the Unseen. At night he will look up to the stars that glitter above the still camp and talk like a theologian, moralizing upon the fact that while God's stars are unerring in their courses God's human creatures are so erratic. But he is no mere dreamer; you may see him, when the enemy is known to be near, sleeping in his saddle, with his gun across it, that he may be no sooner awake than ready. One who knew not of this habit was once imprudent enough to touch him in his sleep, as he wanted to speak to him; he had only time to knock up the swiftly pointed barrel with his hand and John Brown's bullet grazed the intruder's shoulder.

One of the first deeds in this campaign, and the one that certainly first turned the tide and caused the pro-slavery ruffians to feel that they had need to look to their own safety, and would not be suffered with impunity to murder whom they chose and fire honest men's houses like fiends let loose, was the midnight massacre at Pottawatomie. Along a certain creek there lived five of these incendiaries and outrage-mongers who were specially notorious. A report reached Brown that they were sworn to sweep the neighbourhood clear of Abolitionists, not forgetting 'those Browns.' That they were to be kept in terror by such a gang seemed to Brown an unrighteous state of things, and he formed the desperate design of visiting them first. But he loved not slaughter for slaughter's sake. Not only could he strike upon occasion, but he could be just in his rough-and-ready fashion. He argued within himself, 'I shall be right in killing these men if I am sure they intend these murders, but I will not act upon mere report.' Disguising himself, he started with two men to carry a surveyor's chain, and one to carry a flag. No coward was this man. He would put his life in peril rather than act on mere suspicion. So he ran his lines past the houses of these five men, and they naturally came out to see what this surveying business was. Brown told them, as he looked through his instrument and waved the flagman to this side or that, 'Yours is a grand country. Are there many Abolitionists about here?' In his pocket-book he jotted down the answer 'Yes,' and, swearing great oaths, they told him that they meant to sweep the region clear of them in a week. 'Are there some called Brown?' 'Yes,' and man by man they swore the Browns should be killed by their hands. Back he went saying to himself, 'If I understand the Book these are murderers, they have committed murder in their hearts.' Ere many nights were passed eight men were requisitioned from the camp. They stole forth armed with short cutlasses, and next morning the ghastly news spread abroad that five corpses had been found by that creek. John Brown, jun., said, 'The only statement that I ever heard my father make in regard to this was "I did not myself kill any of those men at Pottawatomie, but I am as fully responsible as if I did."' It was a terrible act; we cannot wonder that it came as a great shock to many who had the cause of liberty at heart, but when questioned about it the old man was always reticent, and would only say, 'God is my Judge.'

The result was unmistakable. From that moment John Brown's name became a terror to the evildoers of that quarter. The free settlers felt there was another fate than extermination for them, and the impotent administration at Washington first began to see that this hitherto submissive majority of free settlers must be reckoned with. A writer said years after, 'It was like a clap of thunder from a clear sky.' There are acts that can only be morally estimated by a careful consideration of the prevailing circumstances, and in this case they are such as we, well housed and protected folk, thank God, know not. Those who knew this man through and through were swift to testify, 'Whatever may be thought of John Brown's acts, John Brown himself was right.' No personal end had he to serve; his harvest was privation, suffering, death. He had no personal vengeance to wreak, and when revengeful words were spoken in his hearing he soon lifted the conversation to a sublime level.

'That,' said he, 'is not a Christian spirit. If I thought I had one bit of the spirit of revenge I would never lift my hand. I do not make war on slave-holders, but on slavery.'

Henceforth John Brown's little band was famous. A few days after the Pottawatomie tragedy we find him engaging a company under Captain Fate, who professed, with doubtful authority, to be the emissary of the Government. Hearing after prayer meeting one Sunday they are in the neighbourhood, he is quickly in pursuit as soon as night has set in, and in the morning with a handful of men he is exchanging brisk fire with the enemy. Presently Fred Brown, a wild-looking man of the woods, who has been left in charge of the horses, comes riding upon a pony none too large for its ungainly burden. He waves his long arms, shouting, 'Come on, boys, we've got 'em surrounded and cut off their communications.' The enemy are scared at the apparition, and their captain, thinking there is no fathoming the plots of these Browns, sends a lieutenant forward with a flag of truce. John Brown asks, 'Are you captain!' 'No.' 'I will talk with him, not with you.' Captain Fate advances with much parley. 'Any proposition to make?' impatiently asks John Brown. 'No.' Then he (John Brown) has one—unconditional surrender; and with eight men he has soon secured twenty prisoners. So all through that summer Brown was wellnigh ubiquitous in harassing the enemy, and their dispatches betray their terror of him by ludicrous exaggerations of his achievements. But it is certain he lived as nearly up to his terrible reputation as he could. At Franklin, at Washington Creek, and at Osawatomie we find him in evidence. Here are extracts from his letters in reference to the attack made by the pro-slavery men at the last-mentioned place. 'On the morning of August 30 an attack was made by the ruffians on Osawatomie, numbering some 400, by whose scouts our dear Frederick was shot dead.' (This was his son, and it was by a Methodist preacher's rifle he was killed. Such was the support which the pulpit sometimes gave in those turbulent days to the slavery cause.) 'At this time I was about three miles off, where I had some fourteen or fifteen men overnight that had just enlisted under me. These I collected with some twelve or fifteen more, and in about three-quarters of an hour I attacked them from a wood with thick undergrowth.

'With this force we threw them into confusion for about fifteen or twenty minutes, during which time we killed or wounded from seventy to eighty of the enemy—as they say—and then we escaped as we could with one killed, two or three wounded, and as many more missing. Jason (another son) fought bravely by my side. I was struck by a partly spent shot which bruised me some, but did not injure me seriously. "Hitherto the Lord has helped me, notwithstanding my afflictions."'

Later there was a futile attack upon Lawrence by 2,700 Of the Border ruffians, and while the governor claimed afterwards the credit for the failure of the attack, it is certain that his dilatory intervention had less to do with the result than the prompt action of a couple of hundred defenders of the place who made a dash outwards towards the advancing rabble. Mounted on a grocer's box in the main street, John Brown thus addressed them before action: 'If they come up and attack don't yell, but remain still. Wait till they get within twenty-five yards of you: get a good object: be sure you see the hind sight of your gun—then fire. A great deal of powder and lead is wasted on aiming too high. You had better aim at their legs than at their heads. In either case, be sure of the hind sights of your guns. It is from the neglect of this that I myself have so many times escaped; for if all the bullets that have ever been aimed at me had hit, I should have been as full of holes as a riddle.'

All these skirmishes from a military point of view were trivial, but from a political standpoint they were crucial. They saved Kansas, and made free election at length possible. Brown and his men were 'incarnate earnestness,' says one writer, and it was that fervent devotion which made all that followed possible. It became impossible for a government to wink at arson and murder. 'Take more care to end life well than to live long,' the old man used to say, and he exemplified his doctrine.

His reckless bravery was proverbial. After one of their successful skirmishes a wounded Missourian wished greatly to see the redoubtable John Brown before he died. The captain went to the wagon where he lay and said, 'Here I am; take a good look at me; we wish you all no harm. Stay at home, leave us alone, and we shall be friends. I wish you well.' The dying man looked at him from head to foot, and, reaching out his hand, said, 'I don't see as you are so bad. You don't look or talk like it. I thank you.' Clasping his hand, the old captain said, 'God bless you,' and his tears were the Amen. Thus tender was he ever with his prisoners, despite his fierceness.

At length the United States Government saw the free settlers were in no abject mood, and stepped in to their relief. John Brown saw the dawn of better days, and then travelled away northward, worn and sick, with a fugitive slave as a kind of trophy hidden in his wagon. Before long he found security and peace for a while at North Elba, New York, at the house of Gerrit Smith.

CHAPTER VI
THE UNDERGROUND RAILWAY

We now find John Brown busy for a while in the Northern States addressing Abolitionist meetings, collecting funds for the cause, and co-operating with the Anti-slavery Committees, of which there were several thousands. In many homes where the friends of freedom lived he was a welcome guest, not least welcomed by the children, who always seemed to refresh his weary heart. 'Out of the mouths of children,' as the psalmist says (according to one version), 'God gives strength to true men.' You might often have seen him holding up a little two-year-old child, saying, 'When John Brown is hanged as a traitor she can say she used to stand on John Brown's hand.' He was no false prophet!

Now also he was able to revisit, after two years' absence, the old homestead where his wife and children were awaiting him, down to the little one whom he had left an infant in the cradle. 'Come,' says the strange father to the little prattler, 'I have sung it to all of them; I must sing it to you.'

Blow ye the trumpet, blow
The gladly solemn sound:
Let all the nations know
To earth's remotest bound.
The year of Jubilee is come,
Return, ye ransomed sinners, home.

In strains to which a soul on fire gave enchantment and a tunefulness of their own he sang that song of Moses and the Lamb, telling of the Jewish charter of Liberty to which Christ in His turn gave larger meaning; and the little eyes in the room beheld a transfigured face which they remembered when he had ceased blowing the trumpet of Jubilee, and when they sang the same hymn as they laid him beneath the sod outside that cabin door.

But not long could he stay at home. The year of Jubilee for all these bondmen was his one thought, and he found friends who regarded him as a tried man and were prepared to trust him implicitly. Such men as Beecher and Theodore Parker gave him help spiritual; men like the wealthy Stearns gave him help financial to the extent of many thousand dollars, and were content to know that John Brown, however he spent it (and concerning his plans he was always reticent), would have but one object—liberty to the captive.

One way in which it was spent was in the working of what was then known as the underground railway. The opportunist statesman—Henry Clay—had led many Northern voters to tolerate the passing of the Fugitive Slave Law, under which the Federal Government facilitated the enforced return of fugitive slaves found in free states to the plantations of the South. And the Abolitionists in the North, as a set-off against this detested legislation, gave themselves with much zest to aid the runaway slave. If a slave could escape to the swamps or the forest and elude the bloodhounds on his track, he knew that at certain points he would find those who were prepared to house him, and, passing him on secretly from station to station, ensure his arrival at a terminus where he would be safe for life. That was Canada, the country where the Union Jack waves—the flag of 'Britons' who 'never shall be slaves' and are prepared to grant to all the priceless boon they claim themselves. This escape was called 'shaking the paw of the lion.' May that British lion never be transformed into a sleek tiger; may his paw ever be outreached to a runaway slave, and his roar be a terror to all who would market in human flesh and blood!

This chain of well-known houses and locations was called the underground railway; and, spite of penalties of imprisonment oft inflicted, it never lacked porters or guards; and if the trains did not always run to time it was because they were very cautious against accident. Some 30,000 passengers were probably conveyed on this line. You will not be surprised to find John Brown an active 'guard,' and under the name of 'Shubel Morgan' or 'Hawkins' he did good service there. See him making his way with twelve fugitive slaves from Missouri, through Kansas, Nebraska, Iowa, Illinois, and Michigan to Canada. It is the dead of winter, and the rough wagons travel heavily and slowly along the drifted roads. There is a price on his head in these Southern States—3,250 dollars offered conjointly by the Governor of Missouri and President Pierce—and the stations are sometimes thirty miles apart. They come to a creek, and there is the State Marshal awaiting them with eighty armed men—for he thought he had better have a good force, as he heard it was John Brown he might encounter. John puts his host of twenty-three men all told into battle array in front of the wagons, and gives the laconic order, 'Now go straight at 'em, boys, they are sure to run.' Into the water his men charge—but the baptism of water is all they are fated to pass through; there is no baptism of fire to follow, for, scared at the impulsive charge, and filled with vague terror at that irrepressible John Brown, the Marshal springs upon his horse and skedaddles. His men scramble to their horses. Some cannot untie them from the shrubs quickly enough; several animals carry two men, and, to complete the ludicrousness of the scene, one man, fearing he might be too late, grips fast the tail of the steed to which the proper rider has just set spurs, and, vainly trying to spring on behind, is seen with his feet off the ground, being whirled through the air. A few prisoners are speedily added to Brown's little company, who, thinking it is perhaps prudent to keep men off horseback who were so prone to flight, orders them to walk.

But he has ideas of courtesy, has this rough old warrior, and says he means them no unkindness and will walk with them. Such a favourable opportunity must in no wise be missed, so the old soldier-prophet gives them his mind upon the wickedness of slave-holding and the meanness of slave-hunting, which discourse, let us hope, is not wholly unfruitful. When he has held them for one night he thinks they have been brought far enough from their haunts to prevent further mischief, and sets them free. That one night spent with him they are not likely to forget. He would not so much as allow them the privilege of swearing. 'No taking of God's name in vain gentlemen; if there is a God you will gain nothing, and if there is none you are fools indeed.' Such is the old man's plain argument.

One of them, a harum-scarum young physician, is taken specially under charge by John Brown. Before retiring Brown desires him to pray. 'I can't pray,' he says, with an oath. 'What, did your mother never teach you?' asks Brown. 'Oh yes,' he replies; 'but that was a long time ago.' 'Well, you still remember the prayer she taught you?' continued Brown. 'Yes,' is the answer. 'Say that for want of a better,' is the order. Then, to the amusement of all, the poor doctor repeats the rhyme:

And now I lay me down to sleep,
I pray the Lord my soul to keep.

Said the young doctor after he was released, 'John Brown knows more about religion than any man I ever met. He never used harsh language; we were treated like gentlemen; we shared food with them. Only it went against the grain to be guarded by niggers.'

Thus the journey proceeds. As they get farther north there is more bark than bite about the opposition they encounter. In the street at one town where they are sheltered, Brown strolls alone and finds a champion of slavery haranguing the crowd and denouncing Brown as a reckless, bloody outlaw, a coward who skulked and would never fight in the open. Warming to a climax the orator proclaims, 'If I could get a sight of him I would shoot him on the spot; I would never give him a chance to steal any more slaves.' 'My friend,' says a plain-looking countryman—no other than John Brown himself—on the outskirts of the throng, 'you talk very brave; and as you will never have a better opportunity to shoot old Brown than right here and now, you can have a chance.' But his powder was damped—or his courage!

Now the journey is over. The twelve fugitives have become thirteen, for a little infant has been born on the march, never to know, thank God, the horrors the mother has left behind. The child is named after his deliverer 'John Brown,' who conducts them safely across the ferry and places them under the shelter of the Union Jack on the Canadian shore. Then the old man reverently pronounces his 'Nunc dimittis,' 'Lord, now lettest thou Thy servant depart in peace, for mine eyes have seen Thy salvation.' 'I could not brook the thought that any ill should befall them, least of all that they should be taken back to slavery. The arm of Jehovah has protected us.' Before many months those rescued ones were weeping at the news that John Brown was condemned to die, and were saying 'Would that we could die instead.'

CHAPTER VII
HARPER'S FERRY

John Brown now prepared for his final effort, for the enterprise he had espoused and the sacrifice he had sworn to make for it were to be completed by his death. 'There is no way of deliverance but by blood,' had become his settled conviction upon this slavery question. And truly it seemed so. The Slave States were waxing fiercer in their unholy enterprise. The reopening of the market for freshly imported slaves from Africa was openly advocated—indeed, prices were offered for the best specimens, as if it were a mere cattle trade. 'For sale, 400 negroes just landed,' was placarded in Southern streets; and to complete the grim situation a prize was proposed for the best sermon in defence of the slave trade. Surely the Lord gave not 'the word,' but 'great was the company of the preachers' who were prepared to publish it.

John Brown felt that the fullness of time was come for a desperate stroke. Desperate indeed it was. From a military point of view it was madness. He resolved to hire a farm in Maryland, near to the great armoury at Harper's Ferry in the Slave State of Virginia, and there diligently and silently to store arms. Then with a small company he would seize Harper's Ferry. Having possessed himself of its stores, he would retreat to the mountains, where he hoped there would be considerable rallying to his standard. Holding his own amid mountain fastnesses of which he had acquired an intimate knowledge, he thought he might at last become strong enough to make terms with the Government.

We next find him passing as Isaac Smith, a Maryland farmer—known to his neighbours as a demure, somewhat eccentric, son of the soil. Three of his sons, true to the vow, were with him. Little thought the farmers around that hard by that farmhouse a few thousand weapons were stored and that a little band of mysterious strangers was gathering there, but so it was. To the last there was much opposition to Brown's impulsive scheme. Once, indeed, he resigned leadership, but the little group passed a horrible five minutes of bereavement and then re-elected him with many promises of support. Sublime old madman!—if mad indeed he was! Had he not made them all feel like himself, 'that they have but one life and once to die; and if they lose their lives perchance it will do more for the cause than their lives would be worth in any other way?'

One reluctant darkie, rescued by him from slavery, was challenged to say what he would do. He hesitated—looked at his shaggy old benefactor, and then, with heart surcharged with gratitude, said, 'I believe I'll go wid de ole man.'

Ah! the old man's soul had entered into them—it kept them 'marching on.' In the dark, wet night of October 16, 1859, they mustered quietly. The captain addressed them, and he was no reckless destroyer of human life who thus spake: 'Gentlemen, let me press this one thing on your minds. You all know how dear life is to you, and how dear your lives are to your friends; and in remembering that, consider that the lives of others are as dear. Do not therefore take the life of any one if you can possibly avoid it, but if it is necessary to take life in order to save your own, then make sure work of it.'

Two of them were deputed to hasten, when the town was in their hands, to Colonel Washington's house, four miles distant—to seize him, free his slaves, and take the relic of the house, the famed sword of his illustrious ancestor George Washington, that with this in hand John Brown might head the campaign. That feat they actually performed, and for one brief day their leader bore that sword.

Silently marched that little band of about a score under shelter of the darkness. They had their plans complete, even a Constitution ready framed, should they be successful. The telegraph wires were cut. They contrived to terrify all on guard without firing a shot, and as the sun rose, Harper's Ferry, arsenal, armoury, and rifle works, and many prisoners were in the hands of John Brown. The day wore on, but the expected reinforcements came not; the spreading news, however, brought hostile troops around the captured place, and they hourly increased. Brown took not his one chance of escape to the mountains—why, it is difficult to say. In prison afterwards he said his weakness in yielding to the entreaties of his prisoners ruined him. 'It was the first time I ever lost command of myself, and now I am punished for it,' he added. At another time when questioned he gave fatalistic answers, and said it was 'ordained so ages before the world was made.' By afternoon he was on the defensive within the armoury, and a fierce fight ensued. Even then his simple notions of justice were uppermost, and to the last as his men fired from the portholes he would be heard saying of some one passing in the street, 'That man is unarmed don't shoot.' Two of his sons—Watson and Oliver Brown—were pierced with bullets. As he straightened out the limbs of the second, he said, 'This is the third son I have lost in the cause.' Always the cause! The night fell and the fight was in abeyance, but in the morning he was summoned to surrender, and refused, saying he would die there. At length the engine-house, their last resort, held stubbornly, was captured, and Brown fell, wounded by the sword of a young lieutenant who had marked him for his stroke. One of his prisoners who was by says truly of his last fight, 'Almost any other man who saw his sons fall would have exacted life for life, but he spared all of us who were in his power.' Of the force of twenty-two men, ten were killed, seven captured and hanged, and five escaped. On the other side six were killed and eight wounded.

He was now a captive, suffered to recover from his wounds that he might die a felon's death. Many were those who, from various motives, came to see the wounded prisoner, and from many interviews reported at the time we may take a few extracts:

Q. Can you tell us who furnished money for your expedition?

A. I furnished most of it myself. I cannot implicate others. It is by my own folly I have been taken. I could have saved myself had I not yielded to my feelings.

Q. If you would tell us who sent you, who provided means, it would be valuable information.

A. I will answer freely and faithfully about what concerned myself, anything I can with honour, but not about others. It was my own prompting and that of my Maker or the devil—whichever you please to ascribe it to—I acknowledge no master in human form.

Q. Why came you here?

A. To liberate the slaves—the cry of the oppressed is my only reason. I respect the rights of the poorest coloured folk as much as those of the most wealthy and powerful.

Q. How do you justify your acts?

A. I think, my friend, you are guilty of a great wrong against God and humanity—I say it without wishing to be offensive and it would be perfectly right for any one to free those you wickedly hold in bondage. I am not here to gratify revenge, but because I pity those who have none to help them.

Q. Do you consider this a religious movement?

A. The greatest service man can render to God.

Q. Do you consider yourself an instrument in the hands of Providence?

A. I do.

Q. Brown, suppose you had every nigger in the United States, what would you do with them?

A. Set them free.

Said Governor Wise of Virginia, 'Mr. Brown, the silver of your hair is reddened by the blood of crime, and you should eschew these hard words and think of eternity. You are committing felony by these sentiments.' Brown replied, 'Governor, I have by all appearances not more than fifteen or twenty years the start of you in the journey to eternity, and whether my time has to be long or short I am equally prepared to go. There is an eternity behind and an eternity before, and this speck in the centre, however long, is but comparatively a minute. The difference between your tenure and mine is trifling, and you have all of you a heavy responsibility and it behoves you to prepare more than it does me.'

The Governor's public testimony was: 'They are mistaken who took Brown to be a madman. He is a bundle of the best nerves I ever saw. He is a man of clear head, of courage, fortitude, and simple ingenuousness. He is cool, collected, and indomitable; and it is but just to him to say that he was humane to his prisoners, and he inspired me with great trust in his integrity as a man of truth. He is a fanatic, vain and garrulous, but firm, truthful, and intelligent. He professes to be a Christian in communion with the Congregational Church of the North, and openly preaches his purpose of universal emancipation, and the negroes themselves were to be the agents, by means of arms, led on by white commanders. Colonel Washington says that he was the coolest and firmest man he ever saw in defying danger and death. With one son dead by his side, and another shot through, he felt the pulse of his dying son with one hand, held his rifle with the other, and commanded his men with the utmost composure, encouraging them to be firm, and to sell their lives as dearly as they could.'

The trial for treason and murder took place in the Virginian Court on October 27-31, ere he had recovered. He pleaded for delay till his health allowed him to give more attention to his defence, but the request was refused. So, weak and wounded, he had to lie upon his pallet with a blanket thrown over him. His words were few, and to the same effect as those we have quoted. There was only one verdict possible in that court—GUILTY—and he was sentenced to be hanged. Technically there was no other course possible. The calm verdict of the CAMBRIDGE MODERN HISTORY upon the raid is correct: 'It was the mad folly of an almost crazed fanatic . . . the stain still upon him of the bloodiest of the lawless work done in the name of

Freedom; a terrible outlaw because an outlaw for conscience' sake; intense to the point of ungovernable passion—heeding nothing but his own will and sense of right; a revolutionist upon principle; a lawless incendiary, and yet seeking nothing for himself.'

But while we feel the veracity of these words there comes to our mind one of Charles Kingsley's impulsive sayings: 'Get hold of one truth, let it blaze in your sky like a Greenland sun, never setting day or night. See it in everything, and everything in it. The world will call you a bigot and fanatic, and then fifty years after will wonder how it was the bigot and fanatic managed to do so much more than all the sensible men round about him.'

John Brown vindicated that opinion.

CHAPTER VIII
THE HALT OF THE BODY AND THE MARCH OF THE SOUL

The journeys of John Brown's body were now at an end. Only his soul was free to travel, and it found its vehicle in letters which carried thoughts that breathed and words that burned far and wide.

This condemned prisoner had five weeks left of mortal life, and they were the most fruitful he ever spent. The greatest achievement of his life was the marvellous advocacy of the cause conducted from his prison. His friend F. B. Sanborn says: 'Here was a defeated, dying old man, who had been praying and fighting and pleading and toiling for years, to persuade a great people that their national life was all wrong, suddenly converting millions to his cause by the silent magnanimity or the spoken wisdom of his last days as a fettered prisoner.'

He had spoken of a Samson's victory as possibly the great triumph in store for him. Even so it was, and in his death and by the manner of it he mortally wounded his old enemy, Slavery. As the great continent watched from afar his last days, a thrill passed through it that made Emancipation a triumphant cause. Efforts to save Brown's life might be in vain, but Brown's death was helping to save the life of the nation. His letters from the prison were many and widely circulated. All he has to say of himself is that he knows no degradation. 'I can trust God with the time and manner of my death, believing that for me now to seal my testimony with my life will do vastly more for the Cause than all I have done before. Dear wife and children, do not feel degraded on my account.' Humorously he remarks, 'I am worth inconceivably more to hang than for any other purpose.' 'Say to my poor boys never to grieve for one moment on my account; and should many of you live to see the time when you will not blush to own your relation to old John Brown, it will not be more strange than many things that have happened.' '"He shall BEGIN to deliver Israel out of the hand of the Philistines." This,' said he, 'I think is true of my commission from God and my work.' The scaffold had no terrors for him. His trust, he averred, was firm in that Redeemer who, to European and Ethiopian, bond and free alike, had brought a year of Jubilee and a great salvation. But though he asked no pity for himself, he pleaded in every letter for those who, as he said, were on the 'under-hill' side. 'Weep not for me,' he wrote home, 'but for the crushed millions who have no comforter.' The old text was continually repeated, 'Remember them that are in bonds as bound with them,' and he bade them abhor with undying hatred that 'sum of all villanies—slavery.'

His only cause of agitation in the prison was the intrusive ministration of certain pro-slavery parsons. He refused to let a man who 'had the blood of the slaves on his skirts' minister to him. 'I respect you as a gentleman, but a HEATHEN gentleman,' he would say. 'Don't let such go with me to the scaffold,' he asked. 'I would rather have an escort of barefooted, bareheaded, ragged slave boys and girls led by some old grey-headed slave mother.'

A sculptor who had conceived a great admiration for the brave old man was ambitious to execute a marble bust of him. He applied to Mrs. Stearns—Brown's old wealthy supporter—to aid him in his enterprise. She readily promised to supply all funds, but, said she, 'You will have a vain journey for the measurements. He will just say, "Nonsense; give the money to the poor." You will then say, "Mr. Brown, posterity will want to know what you looked like," and he will reply, "No consequence to posterity how I looked; better give the money to the poor." But go if you will and use my name.' And off went the eager artist. With some difficulty he procured an interview with the prisoner. But woman is far-sighted; sure enough the answer came, 'Nonsense; give the money to the poor.' But the artist pleaded, 'Posterity will want to see what you were like.' Said the man who longed that his work rather than his memory should live, 'No consequence to posterity how I looked; give the money to the poor.' However, the name of Mrs. Steams prevailed at last, and with a thankful look he said, 'She must have what she desires; take the measurements.'

The day of execution, December 2, 1859, drew near. Excitement increased, and for the first time in the history of the Union the passport system was introduced by the State Government of Virginia, and was maintained during the last eight days of Brown's life, lest haply aid from the North should be organized. Troops were present to the number of 3,000, around the scaffold at Charlestown, when he was carried forth to die. Rumour alleged that he had on the way to the scaffold taken a slave child from its mother's arms and kissed it. But, credible as it may have been to many, those who were present knew he was too closely pinioned and guarded for it to be possible. He had little to say—only one word of the glory of the surrounding scenery, for he was a true son of Nature to the last. He had placed in an official's hands a slip of paper with the following words upon it: 'I, John Brown, am now quite certain that the crimes of this guilty land will never be purged away but with blood. I had, as I now think vainly, flattered myself that without very much bloodshed it might be done.'

Upon the scaffold he only bade them be quick, as he was quite ready. Ready! Yes, he had been ready many a year, and it was no unwilling victim that swung mid-air that December morning.

They carried his body to the old log-house he occupied at North Elba, where it was buried upon the farm. That farm has been recently purchased for a public park; and the grave, with the big boulder upon it, forms a conspicuous feature. Thousands approach it with reverent feet, not so much because of the body which lies mouldering there, but for the sake of the soul which is marching on. They had sung in Northern streets a grim ditty during those days of suspense before his execution, with the refrain, addressed to the Southerner:

> And Old Brown, Osawatomie Brown,
> May trouble you more than ever
> When you've nailed his coffin down.

It contains a true word of prophecy. Says an American writer: soon after, 'I meet him at every turn. John Brown is not dead; he is more alive than ever he was.' As that same year the Northern States gird themselves for the great Presidential contest, determined that at length a thorough Abolitionist named Abraham Lincoln shall tenant the White House, it is evident that John Brown's soul is marching on.

When at length fierce civil war breaks out, and those same Northern States month by month are brought to the sure conviction that Freedom as certainly as Union is the cause for which they fight, and as through long disappointment and suspense, lavish effusion of blood, generous sacrifice of their bravest sons they steadily press to victory under the ever-patient, dogged leadership of President Lincoln and General Grant, it is evident that John Brown's soul is marching on.

In the tramp of ten thousands of armed men, in the strains of that grand old battle-hymn of the Republic, I hear the march of his soul:

> Mine eyes have seen the glory of the coming of the Lord:
> He is trampling out the vintage where the grapes of wrath are stored;
> He hath loosed the fateful lightning of His terrible, swift sword:
> His truth is marching on.
> Glory, glory, hallelujah, &c.

He hath sounded forth the trumpet that shall never call retreat;
He is sifting out the hearts of men before His judgement-seat;
Oh, be swift, my soul! to answer Him; be jubilant, my feet!
Our God is marching on.

I have seen Him in the watchfires of a hundred circling camps;
They have builded Him an altar in the evening dews and damps;
I can read His righteous sentence by the dim and flaring lamps;
His day is marching on.

In the beauty of the lilies Christ was born across the sea,
With a glory in His bosom that transfigures you and me:
As He died to make men holy, let us live to make men free!
While God is marching on.

When Lincoln's first Emancipation Decree (made necessary by the fact that so many blacks belonging to the disloyal were fighting for the Union), that all slaves in the Rebel States from New Year's Day, 1863, shall be free, is promulgated; and when, two years later, the Constitution is amended so as to forbid slavery all through the Republic, now again united; when the nation generously provides food, shelter, and education for the emancipated; and when the freed bondmen greet their liberty-loving President in Southern streets with shouts of gratitude and cries of 'Father Abraham'—you may know that John Brown's soul is marching on.

There in America and elsewhere it continues its march. Wherever the swift cruiser speeds in pursuit of the infamous slave-ship, in every heart-beat of the brave seamen who feel they are on a righteous errand and will overhaul her in the King's—aye, in God's—name, we hear the march of John Brown's soul.

When a nation of free men rises up in wrath at the issue of some official document that seems to be couched in temporizing language on this supreme subject, or at some government that has tolerated conditions that approximate slavery, and will have none of it, we know the old hero's soul is marching on.

Whenever in secret council the ambassador of a free people negotiates a treaty, and, backed by the most sacred impulses of those he represents, urges an anti-slavery clause, we know John Brown's soul is on the march.

And march it shall, while nations learn to prize liberty as God's great chartered right to every man, while they read the shining letters of the Golden Rule, while they remember that God made all men of one blood and that all are redeemed by the blood of One.

While God looks down from His heaven and sees the distressed face, or hears the piercing cry of the oppressed, and can turn the hearts of men to fight His battles upon earth, the soul of John Brown will be marching still.